Loneliness Remover

T5-ADP-200

Also by Michael Krawetz
SELF-ESTEEM PASSPORT

Loneliness Remover

MICHAEL KRAWETZ

An Owl Book
Henry Holt and Company
New York

Copyright © 1988 by Michael Krawetz.
All rights reserved, including the right to reproduce
this book or portions thereof in any form.
Published by Henry Holt and Company, Inc.,
115 West 18th Street, New York, New York 10011.
Published in Canada by Fitzhenry & Whiteside Limited,
195 Allstate Parkway, Markham, Ontario L3R 4T8.

Library of Congress Cataloging-in-Publication Data
Krawetz, Michael.
Loneliness remover.
"An Owl book."
1. Loneliness.   2. Conduct of life.   I. Title.
BF575.L7K73   1988   158'.2   88-9480
ISBN 0-8050-0363-0 (pbk.)

Henry Holt books are available at special discounts for bulk
purchases for sales promotions, premiums, fund raising, or
educational use. Special editions or book excerpts can also be
created to specification.

    For details, contact:

    Special Sales Director
    Henry Holt and Company, Inc.
    115 West 18th Street
    New York, New York 10011

First Edition

Designed by Victoria Hartman
Printed in the United States of America
10 9 8 7 6 5 4 3 2 1

With special thanks to Marilyn Lehr, Connie Kaiser,
and Lil Albrecht for their continued support
and encouragement.

This book is dedicated to the memory of Lance Corporal Jack Wolpe of Newburgh, New York, a fallen Vietnam hero.

"The one cruel fact about heroes is that they are made up of flesh and blood."
—Henry Arthur Jones

Contents

Preface: Why *Loneliness Remover*? ix

How *Loneliness Remover* Works 1

Your Loneliness Remover Contract 2

How to Strengthen Your Self-Esteem to Win Over Loneliness 5

How to Create an Improved Physical Self-Image in Five Minutes 6

How to Strengthen Your Self-Confidence to Remove Loneliness 8

Why Your Former Disappointments Will Strengthen Your Self-Esteem 10

Why Risk-Taking Increases Your Self-Esteem and Pushes Away Loneliness 12

How to Become Your Own Best Friend and Attract Others 14

How to Classify Your Type of Loneliness 16

How to Triumph Over Your Shyness 19

Why Rejection Can Be a Strengthening Process 22

Why a Trustworthy Listener Will Lighten Your Loneliness 24

Why Helping Someone Else Reduces Your Loneliness 26

How to Break Your Addiction to Loneliness 28

Why Owning a Pet Reduces Your Loneliness 30

How Religion Can Help You Overcome Loneliness 32

How to Transcend the Loneliness of Mourning 34

How to Overcome the Loneliness of the Workplace 36

Why Excessive TV Viewing Will Prolong Your Loneliness 38

How to Meet Friends You Still Haven't Met 40

Why the Search for Perfection Can Increase Loneliness 42

How to Rekindle Old Friendships to Remove Loneliness 44

Why Sharing Your Home Removes Loneliness 46

Why Casual Sex Can Prolong Your Loneliness 48

Why You Should Detach from a Lonely Friendship 50

How to Avoid Loneliness in Retirement 52

How Temporary Work Can Help You Find New Friends 54

How to Use Personal Ads to Remove Your Loneliness 56

How to Avoid Being Lonely in a Relationship 58

How to Avoid the Holiday Cycle of Loneliness and Depression 60

How to Stop the Loneliness of Overdrinking or Overeating 62

Why Adult Education Courses Yield New Friends 64

Why Group Therapy Is a Powerful Remedy for Loneliness 66

How Not to Suffer the Loneliness of an Alcoholic Relationship 68

How to Defeat Teenage Loneliness 71

How to Avoid the Loneliness of Motherhood 74

How Newspapers Can Help You Beat Loneliness 76

How to Beat the Loneliness of Overspending 78

How to Beat the Loneliness of Machismo 80

Why It's Time to Throw Your Own Party 82

To the Special People Who Read My Book 85

Preface: Why *Loneliness Remover?*

Someone had to write this book.

Someone who experienced the loneliness of feeling unloved. Someone who understood the despair of the friendless.

Someone who remembered the plunge into low self-worth touched off by the inability to form or maintain a meaningful personal relationship.

Someone who was once afraid to face another tomorrow because all it represented was another futile twenty-four-hour cycle of more loneliness and self-rejection.

I knew that I would have to write *Loneliness Remover* because I had brought my own loneliness to an end. I had also shown others how to appreciate the precious dignity of personal worth through my first book, the *Self-Esteem Passport*.

I wanted this new book to be special. It would have to be compassionate, inspirational, interactive, and easy to use. And I also hoped that *Loneliness Remover* would become a book for people of all ages and backgrounds, and that it could produce immediate positive results that would last for a lifetime.

No more loneliness.

—*Michael Krawetz*

> "And God stepped out on space,
> And he looked around and said,
> 'I'm lonely—
> I'll make me a world.'"
> —James Weldon Johnson

How *Loneliness Remover* Works
It provides people-connection strategies to overcome isolation.

Regardless of the loneliness pain you're experiencing—whether it's because you lack closeness with another person, feel isolated in your community, or are stuck in a lonely job or relationship—your loneliness can be classified, treated, and corrected. It's that simple.

By following the people-connection strategies found in the pages of this book, you will feel a powerful transformation process begin. By honestly completing the opening personal inventory sections, you will gradually change into a happier, more lovable and self-fulfilled person. These sections are also helpful and fun. Follow the directions carefully, page by page, and you'll enjoy a new growth-building process that's essential to creating anti-loneliness momentum.

With your new self-awareness—and your commitment to refrain from self-condemnation, pessimism, and self-pity—you will be poised to defeat loneliness.

Your loneliness recovery timetable will vary according to your personal commitment, dedication, and enthusiasm—and the amount of time it will take for you to discover how to become your own best friend.

Now the Loneliness Remover process begins:

> "The experience of being loved, of knowing that someone cares for you, that you matter to someone else is the greatest antidote to loneliness."
> —Frieda Fromm Reichmann

Your Loneliness Remover Contract

Sign the contract to upgrade your personal, social, and friendship opportunities.

You took an important first step to rid yourself of loneliness when you made the decision to own a copy of *Loneliness Remover*. You're now ready to improve the quality of your life.

Your next step requires a personal and honest commitment: a contract with yourself to improve your personal, social, and friendship possibilities. The goals are really quite simple to accomplish with this book as your guide.

On the facing page, validate the Loneliness Remover Contract with yourself by writing your name and today's date. Then enter one primary and two secondary goals that you'd like to accomplish in the next thirty days. You may want to refer to the table of contents to select specific goals you wish to achieve.

Keep your goals reasonable and within reach—and stick to your contract. Achieve just one goal or perhaps all three during the first month, and you'll know that you have what it takes to beat loneliness. Realizing just one new anti-loneliness goal will strengthen your self-esteem and provide you with the energizing momentum to defeat loneliness. Accomplish three goals and you may take *loneliness* right out of your vocabulary!

> "The deepest need of man is to overcome his separateness to leave the prison of his aloneness."
> —Erich Fromm

LONELINESS REMOVER CONTRACT*

My primary anti-loneliness goal is _____

_____

My two secondary anti-loneliness goals are _____

_____

_____

Signature and today's date _____

*This contract is not valid unless signed by the owner of this book.

> "It is necessary to the happiness of man that he be mentally faithful to himself."
> —Thomas Paine

How to Strengthen Your Self-Esteem to Win Over Loneliness
A strong self-image will help you attract many new friends.

A positive sense of self-esteem—the way you feel about yourself—is an important personal asset that will provide you with the strength, confidence, and momentum you'll need to remove loneliness from your life.

If you don't like or respect yourself—or are unable to grasp your own self-worth because you've experienced disappointments—those negative feelings about yourself will only reinforce your loneliness. You won't feel good enough about yourself to meet other people. They, in turn, may view you as a loser because of the poor self-image you project.

A strong self-image will enable you to place yourself in new social situations to broaden your friendship possibilities; a weak self-image will keep you trapped in loneliness gridlock. How you feel about yourself will determine your success or failure as a person who no longer wants to remain lonely.

Your newly discovered strengths and capabilities will serve as a powerful magnet to attract others to you in conversation and social interaction. You'll be totally equipped with powerful self-knowledge and new social skills to become a self-fulfilled person brimming with confidence in all circumstances.

And before you're about to embark on a blind date, a new job interview, a Parents Without Partners dance, or a small house party where you may not know anyone except the hostess, be sure to review the contents of the appropriate sections of this book. In fact, memorize and internalize them—they'll provide you with powerful insights and emotional strengths during this new chapter in your life.

The following confidence-building activities—when completed in your handwriting—will reaffirm and revitalize your own strengths and capabilities to meet and conquer all loneliness challenges awaiting you. You are a very special person. You are the key to your own Loneliness Remover achievements. Now let's start by concentrating on your unique self-image.

How to Create an Improved Physical Self-Image in Five Minutes

You're a very special and unique person—there's no one else like you.

The first Loneliness Remover confidence-building action you'll take to strengthen your important self-image is to view yourself as an attractive, acceptable, and appealing person. Remember, how you feel about yourself—and the image of yourself that you project to others—will determine your success or failure in overcoming loneliness. Self-acceptance is a great morale-builder.

Paste a recent photograph of yourself, one that makes you feel good about yourself, in the box opposite. Then list at least three reasons why you're a very special-looking person. There's no other person in the world who looks like you—or even has your particular appeal. Never forget that you're a unique human being.

If you feel too humble or modest to fill in this self-image–building section by yourself, turn to someone you trust to help you describe your physical attributes. Memorize and internalize the responses. Remember, no self-putdowns for being too young, old, short, tall, heavy, or thin. Accepting all your features strengthens your self-esteem. You are the key to your own self-acceptance.

(Example: "I have pretty brown eyes and shiny silver hair that make me look special and appealing. My eyebrows send quite a message.")

(1) _____

(2) _____

(3) _____

Paste a favorite photograph of yourself here.

"Self-confidence is the first requisite to great undertakings."
—Samuel Johnson

How to Strengthen Your Self-Confidence to Remove Loneliness

Your diverse and unique abilities will attract others to you.

The second Loneliness Remover confidence-building action you'll take is to create your self-confidence inventory. By completing this section, you'll be able to project a stronger and more accomplished image of yourself in new situations.

You'll become more attractive and interesting to others by talking about your particular life-mastery skills and accomplishments. What do you do well that others would find interesting about you? What are some of your talents that you're proud of and that reinforce your self-worth as a very competent person?

For example, are you a good cook, home decorator, broken-appliance fixer, or household organizer? Are you very proficient in the work you do—and what about your swimming, gardening, or card-playing skills? Did you ever win any awards in high school or college, or on your job for attaining a specific goal? What are you best at?

In this section, list at least three of your special skills, abilities, or accomplishments that will demonstrate to you—and to others you'll soon be meeting—that you're a uniquely interesting person. Remember, the more in touch you are with your real skills and talents, the more emotional energies and momentum you'll have to embark successfully on new challenges to help you defeat loneliness. Your personal accomplishments will strengthen your self-esteem and help attract others to you.

*(**Example:** "I bake the best monkey bread west of the Mississippi, and can take apart a Ford V-8 engine practically blindfolded—and then put it back together again. I can even jog ten miles without stopping!")*

(1) _____
_____
(2) _____
_____
_____
(3) _____
_____
_____
_____

> "Because a thing seems difficult for you, do not think it is impossible for anyone to accomplish. But whatever is possible for another, believe that you, too, are capable of it."
>
> —Marcus Aurelius

Why Your Former Disappointments Will Strengthen Your Self-Esteem
See them as important turning points in your life that made you stronger.

The third Loneliness Remover confidence-building action, which you're now ready for, is immediately to stop condemning yourself for past disappointments that still fuel the loneliness you feel.

Instead of blaming yourself for those unhappy events that you couldn't control—an engagement or marriage that didn't work out; or the unexpected death of a loved one, which produced survivor's guilt and prolonged mourning—stop letting those grim experiences rob you of any more of your precious self-esteem. The longer you hold on to those painful disappointments, the more lethargic and emotionally weakened you'll become. You'll also deplete yourself of energizing optimism and hope for the future. Transform all of those painful and unhappy memories into constructive self-image builders that will help you smash through loneliness gridlock. See them as important turning points in your life.

You survived a very stressful period. You became more courageous, more self-reliant, and wiser—and practically all by yourself. Endorse yourself for passing through one of life's important milestones with your head held up high. You are a very special and brave person.

By completing this powerful section honestly, you will enable an amazing self-esteem–healing process to take place. In your own words, you'll see how you now refuse to let former disappointments stop you. You'll see that you've always had the determination to triumph over adversity, and that's why you're strong enough to push through all loneliness barriers (real or imagined) standing in your way to self-fulfillment.

In this section, recall three former disappointments that you have surmounted, and explain how those temporary setbacks helped you develop into a stronger and more self-reliant person. Remembering those responses will show you that you have the stamina and determination that it takes to push through future challenges to defeat loneliness.

(Example: "After my marriage ended, I didn't think I could raise my children on my own. I've turned out to be a loving single parent, proud of my independence, and a pretty good breadwinner, too. I won't let the past interfere with my present-day happiness.")

(1) _____

_____

(2) _____

_____

(3) _____

_____

_____

_____

_____

> "To fight aloud is very brave,
> But gallanter, I know,
> Who charge within the bosom,
> The cavalry of woe."
> —Emily Dickinson

Why Risk-Taking Increases Your Self-Esteem and Pushes Away Loneliness
Taking rational risks will add new momentum to your life.

The fourth Loneliness Remover confidence-building action shows you why the previous risks you took now actually serve to strengthen your present self-image. It also demonstrates that you're courageous enough to take additional risks—such as putting yourself into new social situations to attract new people into your life—which should help remove your loneliness.

The willingness to take risks means you are powerful enough to experience change—and are also strong enough to deal with the consequences, successful or not, of your behavior.

In fact, choosing to risk will actually determine your success or failure as a person who is determined not to remain lonely. And even if some of your risks don't result in instant successes, you'll still feel better about yourself, knowing you took an action to improve the quality of your life. You weren't immobilized by fear of change.

Now reach deep into your memory bank and recall your former risk-taking triumphs. Do you remember the time you switched jobs to make yourself feel better by earning more money?

And how about the time you risked buying that new car? You pushed aside those nagging financial fears and succeeded in enjoying the pleasure of your new car purchase.

And what about when you risked going on vacation all by yourself? It was a little difficult at first—but you returned home an accomplished self-sufficient vacationer. You had the strengths and capabilities to take charge of your own life.

In this section, recall three former risk-taking experiences that opened you up to new and expanded opportunities or that helped make your life more satisfying. Explain why those past successes are still powerful enough to provide you with additional momentum to take new risks to push loneliness out of your life.

(Example: "I left the known comfort of a small town to work in a big city even though everyone warned me not to risk leaving home. Choosing to risk turned my life around for the better. I returned stronger, more mature—and had learned to stand on my own. Risk-taking changed my life for the better.")

(1) _____

_____

(2) _____

_____

(3) _____

_____

_____

_____

> "It is only by risking our persons from one hour to another that we live at all."
>
> —William James

How to Become Your Own Best Friend and Attract Others
You'll emerge with a new sense of self-reliance to win over others.

The fifth and final Loneliness Remover confidence-building section in this part of the book will provide you with the insights to help you become your own best friend. You'll also develop a happier and stronger self-image. If you can learn how to do nice things for yourself—and not feel unhappy about being alone or unattached—you'll immediately decrease your vulnerability to social helplessness. By taking individual actions to nourish and improve your life, you'll soon emerge with a new sparkle that will attract others to you.

This immediate-action process begins when you stop all self-condemnation for being alone. This is a key self-acceptance strategy: Don't blame yourself.

Begin liking and appreciating yourself for the way you are—but remain receptive to new opportunities for self-improvement. That's an effective strategy to become your own best friend. Take one or more actions to show the pride that you have in yourself—and that you're someone special.

Treat yourself to good food, clothing, entertainment, or to the pursuit of a favorite hobby. Make the most of your talents. Cook for friends or make a pact with yourself to appreciate all of your unique qualities. Remember, there's no one else like you.

Make a long-distance call to an out-of-town friend. Take out the health club membership you've been postponing. Sign up for an evening course to put more momentum into your life. Take yourself to the best hairstylist in town—and have a manicure at the same time. And how about a short vacation trip to your favorite place?

The more treats you give yourself, the more your life will continue to expand with self-fulfillment and happiness. And as you become your own best friend, your self-esteem will grow to new and stronger levels. You'll purge yourself of the self-condemning feelings that you're no one because you're alone. Your newfound self-reliance will give you a new charisma.

In this section, list three self-initiated and enjoyable

activities you have in store for yourself. Remember, the better the relationship you have with yourself, the more appealing others will find you.

(Example: "I'm through putting my life on hold until the right person comes along. First, I'm buying that new stereo for myself. Next, I'm going out for a five-course meal all by myself. And I think it's about time to look at that nifty Mustang convertible. Now, for tomorrow, there's a really good movie I want to see.")

(1) _____

_____

(2) _____

_____

(3) _____

_____

"The man who goes alone can start today; but he who travels with another must wait till that other is ready."
—Henry David Thoreau

How to Classify Your Type of Loneliness
There are four different and treatable loneliness conditions.

There are four types of loneliness conditions that may affect people during different stages of their lives. They are loneliness of the unloved, loneliness of the friendless, loneliness of self-repudiation, and loneliness of the frantic.

If you're suffering from *loneliness of the unloved*, you're probably unhappy because you don't share a deep relationship with a lover, spouse, or mate.

If you're experiencing *loneliness of the friendless*, you most likely feel alienated because you lack friends and don't know where you fit into your community.

If you're feeling *loneliness of self-repudiation*, it's because you're punishing yourself with self-inflicted negative messages that will further batter your already weakened self-esteem.

If you're affected by *loneliness of the frantic*, you're probably overwhelmed by your current inability to find and connect with others, and you may have turned to drugs or alcohol or other addictions to escape from your painful reality. Compulsive gambling or spending are other examples of this isolating behavior.

Each of the above loneliness conditions is treatable, and the treatment may produce a happy result if the appropriate Loneliness Remover strategies are carried out with full commitment, dedication, enthusiasm, and the courage to push through any latent or overt fear of success.

In order to triumph over any of the four loneliness conditions, it is first crucial to complete and internalize the five-part self-esteem–building process that begins on page 6.

Here's how to win over *loneliness of the unloved*: Now that you feel more likable because of your increased self-esteem, are you up to flirting to attract others? Would you also consider modifying your search for the perfect partner so that you'll produce a much more realistic result? Are you open to a workplace romance—or taking out a classified advertisement to find a new partner?

To defeat *loneliness of the friendless*, start by rekindling an old friendship (page 44), and refer to the section on reaching out to someone less fortunate than yourself (page 26) to help take the emphasis off your isolation. Check the table of contents for other friendship-building sections.

To eliminate *loneliness of self-repudiation*, it is essential to connect with people who will love you until you learn to love yourself. Turn to the sections on becoming part of a group therapy support system (page 66) or attending open meetings of Alcoholics Anonymous, Overeaters Anonymous, or other groups (pages 60 and 62) to experience the principles of sharing and nurturing that repair shattered self-worth, regardless of actual cause. Then implement any other Loneliness Remover strategies that appear comfortable for you to undertake.

To purge yourself of *loneliness of the frantic*, your first assignment is to find a nonjudgmental person to talk to each day; that person may be available through the organization that deals with your particular problem. You need help to keep you centered, slow down your compulsive behavior, and make you feel less lonely, and this help comes from someone who shows concern about your welfare.

In this section, classify the type of loneliness you'd like to overcome, and list three immediate-action strategies you can undertake to help end your loneliness.

(Example: "I'm hindered by the loneliness of self-repudiation. If I don't like myself, why should anyone else? First, I'll work on liking myself and I'll find a trustworthy listener to talk to each day. I'm also going to sign up for a nighttime cooking course to meet some new women friends.")

(1) _____
_____
(2) _____
_____
(3) _____
_____
_____

"Even the woodpecker owes his success to the fact that he uses his head and keeps pecking away until he finishes the job he starts."
—Coleman Cox

"Success begins with a fellow's will—
It's all in the state of mind."
—Walter D. Wintle

How to Triumph Over Your Shyness
Keep your focus on other people and remember how special you are.

Shyness is another form of self-repudiation that will prolong your loneliness and may cause others to see you as unfriendly until you learn how to reduce your self-inflicted fears of meeting others. Regardless of the origins of your shyness—whether it was developed in childhood as a defense to avoid competitive social pressures, or inherited as a family or cultural trait—it can be managed and eventually dispelled.

All you have to do is make an honest commitment to overcome your shyness and pledge not to retreat from any new social situation that could trigger some of your old anxiety behaviors.

The more times you stand up to your timidity and fight to conquer your outmoded childhood coping defenses, by meeting with new people rather than retreating from them, the more you'll create a new emotional strength that will eventually overwhelm your shyness. You'll experience a new emotional initiative that has no boundaries.

The following is a list of shyness-breakers that will strengthen your social and emotional performances when meeting new people or when attending a party or conference where you probably won't know the other people. Follow these procedures and watch your friendships multiply:

STEP ONE: It is important to recognize that, even though they may not show it, the majority of people suffer from shyness, due to their own feelings of imperfection and inadequacy. They're apprehensive because they want you to be interested in them, so stop thinking of them as superior to you and end your nervousness about meeting others.

STEP TWO: Work to overcome your shyness by strengthening your self-esteem. Unless you believe in your own self-worth, you'll always feel inferior, awkward, and nervous about meeting new people. Complete, memorize, and internalize the five-part self-esteem-building section starting on page 6.

STEP THREE: Use the power of your extraordinary mind to visualize and project your next upcoming social success. If you're going on a blind date, visualize just how terrific and likable you're going to be that evening. The more fun and achievements you produce in your visualizations, the more your imaginary momentum will carry over into real life.

STEP FOUR: Don't be self-centered when meeting new people. Shift your thoughts and attention from yourself to them. That outward emphasis will eliminate most of your self-centered anxiety and enhance your personal appeal: Everyone likes attentive listeners; they make a speaker feel important.

STEP FIVE: If you're about to mingle in a new social environment, but you still have some apprehension about speaking to new people, select someone of your sex to talk to. You'll minimize your initial nervousness and build the momentum to begin conversations with members of the opposite sex.

STEP SIX: Prepare an agenda of small-talk items before going to a party or other social functions by reading a newspaper or magazine or listening to several radio and TV news broadcasts to improve your awareness of current affairs. That knowledge will provide you with many new opportunities to start or continue a conversation.

STEP SEVEN: Just try to be yourself in new social situations and don't try to impress others by being different from what you really are. It's easier to be yourself and you won't have to experience internal dishonesty and self-critical thoughts in order to win another person's acceptance.

STEP EIGHT: Share with someone who understands your resolve to win out over shyness the fact that you're going face to face in a new social situation, and that you're committed to overcome your self-imposed jitters no matter how great your fears may be. By sharing your determination with another trusted listener, you won't feel so vulnerable and alone in that new social setting, and you'll also have that special momentum and backing to carry out your goal.

In this section, apply whatever of the above-mentioned shyness-breaking strategies you believe may help you to reduce your fears of meeting others.

(*Example:* "Now that I know that many people are also shy and are worried that I won't be interested in them, I'm changing my philosophy about meeting others. I'm taking the focus off myself, because that eliminates whatever self-doubt I have, and I'll encourage new people I meet to talk about themselves. I have to remember how special and unique I am—no matter how shy I may feel initially.")

_____
_____
_____
_____
_____
_____

> "In all things, success depends upon previous preparation, and without such preparation, there is sure to be failure."
>
> —Confucius

Why Rejection Can Be a Strengthening Process
Each experience will bring you closer to your real people-connection goal.

Rejection can serve as a life-renewal force—and bring you closer to your goal of reaching others—if you don't twist another person's refusal to accept you into a self-repudiating attack on your own character and integrity. See what your exclusion by another person actually represents: Your life experiences, uniqueness, personality, or appearance simply do not happen to fit another person's requirements.

Why allow someone's nonacceptance of your precious individuality to make you feel any less of a person? That's unnecessarily self-punishing behavior. Instead, use that rejection experience to nurture your self-esteem by searching for the real reasons you were rejected by the other person.

For example, you might have experienced rejection because, though highly attracted to you, the other person was so fearful of intimacy and commitment that *you* were rejected strictly because of your availability and the other person's fear of closeness. You could have been rejected because you were really an innocent victim of another person's self-loathing, perfectionist standards.

You also might have been rejected because your features mildly resemble one of your rejector's abusive parents, or even because the other person harbors a latent dislike to all persons of the opposite sex. Or you might have experienced rejection because a financial opportunist—who really wasn't interested in you to begin with—passed you up for another candidate with higher net worth.

Sometimes you may also experience rejection because people may be uncomfortable with your religious beliefs, your sense of humor, the way you dress, or your emotional and social priorities. If that's the case, you can either modify your behavior—without rejecting yourself—or seek out other people who might be less critical of your standards and individuality. That's how to transform rejection into a strengthening experience.

Always keep in mind that your rejection by another probably had nothing to do with you as a person—but only serves as a reflection of someone else's unrealistic expectations.

In this section, produce three solid reasons why another person's rejection of your individual essence should not define you as any less of a good person. Can you discover any latent or hostile reason why you recently faced a rejection from another person?

(Example: "Murphy says he's breaking our engagement because I'm overweight and hate Sunday TV football games. That's not the real reason. He's afraid of growing up, he can't even hold onto a simple job. My weight is fine—his self-esteem isn't. Besides, I'd be happier with a man who'd like visiting museums on Sunday.")

(1) _____

(2) _____

(3) _____

> "The greatest thing in the world is to know how to belong to oneself."
>
> —Michel de Montaigne

Why a Trustworthy Listener Will Lighten Your Loneliness
You will no longer remain isolated in your thoughts.

Reaching out to a trusted friend, family member, or any other nurturing listener—or even to another empathetic person who like you is attempting to conquer loneliness—is a healing activity that will provide you with further incentive to achieve greater happiness. Confiding with someone on a daily basis—in person, on the telephone, or by letter—is an important psychological weapon in your struggle against alienation. Your new confidant—who will provide you with a shoulder to lean on during some of your difficult moments—must be understanding and nonjudgmental and must treat you with dignity.

Here's how that emotionally healing process works: By taking the risk and initiative to find a trustworthy listener who will be there for you on a daily basis, you will no longer feel isolated or out of touch.

Bring yourself to talk about your thoughts and feelings—and even discuss a laughable incident in your life with your confidant. That one-on-one connection will produce an important bond that will help dissolve any feelings that you're unlovable or unacceptable, especially when your trusted listener responds with empathy.

In this section, write down the names of several persons you believe might accept the role of trustworthy listener in this period of your life. Avoid negative and condemning persons who will only make you feel worse about yourself when you reach out to them.

(Example: "I can't afford to be alone in my antisocial behavior. I'm going to reach out to my kid brother. If that doesn't work, perhaps my pastor can recommend someone, or I'll talk to the friendly widower down the block.")

"Nothing is there more friendly to a man than a friend in need."

—Plautus

Why Helping Someone Else Reduces Your Loneliness

You'll be happier with yourself as a result of extending aid to another person.

Caring about others—and doing something thoughtful for someone less fortunate than yourself—will increase your self-confidence, reduce your loneliness, and transform your self-centeredness into a new channel of personal strength and self-fulfillment. The simple actions of cheering a sick friend, helping a stranger carry heavy packages through a busy intersection, or listening to an elderly person's lament will provide you with the emotional rewards of selflessness.

In fact, the more useful deeds you perform for others, the better you'll feel about yourself, and eventually others will take notice of your unselfish traits and your people-to-people concerns. Your loneliness and missing sense of purpose should eventually disappear—and you'll always be important in the eyes of those you reach out to help. Helping others provides an extraordinary feeling of self-worth and acceptance that money can't buy.

In this section, list three direct-action steps you can take to help make the world a better place for someone else.

(Example: "I'm going to visit some disabled World War II veterans in the VA hospital. They've been forgotten by most people. I'll also run some shopping errands for the elderly widow in the neighborhood, and I'll donate some of my old clothing and time to the shelter for battered women. It's time that I put the focus on other people—and not on my loneliness!")

(1) _____
_____
(2) _____
_____
(3) _____
_____
_____

"So many gods, so many creeds
 So many paths that wind and wind,
 When just the art of being kind
Is all this sad world needs."
                    —Ella Wheeler Wilcox

How to Break Your Addiction to Loneliness
Make a conscious decision to give up your self-defeating defense tactics.

Loneliness can become addictive and create habitual depression, alienation, and self-pity. Your addiction to loneliness will serve as an ironclad defense against intimacy, making good relationships impossible. Symptoms of confirmed loneliness addiction include: fear of taking risks, abject shyness, severe fear of rejection, avoidance of all people-connection opportunities, and refusal to learn new social skills. Severe loneliness addiction will also produce rejection or negative responses from peers and potential mates. It can make you into an unhappy recluse with a bleak view of the world.

Some lonely people may experience serious physical and emotional stresses—caused by the absence of friends and by continued depression and negative thinking. The combined setbacks of physical and emotional deprivation in loneliness addicts may reduce their normal life-expectancy rate.

Loneliness addiction is curable; it can be stopped with drastic action. The first step required to stop the negative thinking process is taken by making a conscious decision and honest effort to end this addiction. It means acknowledging to yourself, and to others, that because you were addicted to loneliness it was easier for you to go through life feeling sorry for yourself and withdrawing than to reach out to others for friendship and intimacy.

To break your addiction to loneliness successfully, you must also vow that you'll no longer be bullied by your own fear of rejection. See rejection for what it really is: a learning opportunity for improving your social skills and creating a power-building catalyst that will bring you closer to the kind of people you'd really like to meet—and those who would enjoy your company.

In this section, list three immediate-action steps you can take to help smash your addiction to loneliness if you recognize that trait in yourself.

(Example: "I've hidden from life in recent times because I was too afraid of risking rejection by asking someone out for a date. I'm through taking rejection personally. My new priorities are computer dating, ballroom dancing, and a fun night-school class. I deserve to put new people into my life.")

(1) _____

(2) _____

(3) _____

"Life was meant to be lived, and curiosity must be kept alive. One must never, for whatever reason, turn his back on life."

—Eleanor Roosevelt

Why Owning a Pet Reduces Your Loneliness
Pets are ready-made sources of unselfish love and companionship.

Whether it's a friendly, tail-wagging dog that affectionately jumps up to greet you when you arrive home, or a gentle, playful, purring cat that expresses itself by rubbing against your leg, pets will provide you with instant and effective companionship to reduce your loneliness.

Dogs and cats are extraordinary loneliness removers. They provide constant, unselfish love and friendship. Their totally uncritical devotion is difficult to find in humans. These special friends who depend on you for love, care, and protection will never abandon or betray you, even during the hard times. They'll comfort you when you're depressed, lonely, or worried. Their eyes will reflect the concern they have for you. They will love being hugged. And if you decide to cry in their presence because life sometimes seems so cruel and overwhelming, they won't be judgmental. In fact, they'll even crawl under the covers with you if you ask them.

And if you yell at them during a moment of misplaced anger, they'll never hold a grudge against you. They'll continue demonstrating their love for you—faithful, patient, and unconditional.

Your pet can also serve as your new social link to other people. Take your dog on a walk, and it will introduce you to other animal lovers who have the potential to become new friends. Cats can be a great subject of conversation, too, even if most don't like to go for walks.

And if you live in an environment that doesn't allow you to have a dog or a cat, consider the option of a well-stocked tank of tropical fish. It's soothing to watch fish; they don't have to be walked, and they will swim in your direction out of curiosity and out of their dependence on you to feed them. Or consider buying a parakeet. A colorful little charmer, it will be easy to care for and can be taught how to talk. A cheerful canary is another good companion.

In this section list an immediate-action strategy you

can take to reduce your loneliness through the adopt-a-pet option.

(Example: "*It makes sense for me to own a dog. I'd have extra security at night and great companionship during the day. I'm going to the animal shelter tomorrow to discover a faithful new friend!*")

_____
_____
_____
_____
_____
_____

"Animals are such agreeable friends—they ask no questions, they pass no criticisms."
—George Eliot

How Religion Can Help You Overcome Loneliness
It will provide you with compassion, community, and acceptance.

A strong commitment to your religion, regardless of the faith you observe, may provide you with numerous opportunities to end your loneliness. By strengthening your dedication to your faith and becoming an active member of your respective congregation, parish, or assembly, you may experience a new feeling of family and belonging. Fellow worshippers, including your minister, priest, or rabbi, will usually reach out to establish a special and accepting relationship with you.

And should you feel overwhelmed by a particular burden or problem that may appear painfully hopeless to you, you can also reach out to that same minister, priest, or rabbi. That compassionate servant of God will serve as your friend, confidant, and counselor and will help guide you through your difficulties with prayer, counseling, and compassion.

Religious belief may also help reduce your feelings of alienation during times of stress and self-doubt. By strengthening your link to God through prayer and meditation, you'll create an unstoppable spiritual connection that will be with you wherever you go. You'll never feel alone.

And if you're true to the basic tenets of your faith and reach out to help others who are less fortunate than you, you'll gradually become less preoccupied with your own problems. That focus on others should help transform you into a more fulfilled, happier person. In fact, you may eventually serve as a beacon of hope and inspiration for others who may turn to you as a living example of the power of faith and perseverance.

In this section, determine whether dedicating or rededicating yourself to a faith and attending regular prayer services might help provide you with a feeling of belonging.

(Example: "My religion is important to me, but I've lost touch with my church. I feel God's presence wherever I go, and by reconnecting with other members of the congregation—and confiding in my clergyman—I might build an extended support network.")

_____
_____
_____
_____
_____
_____

> "Nobody can deny but religion is a comfort to the distressed; a cordial to the sick, and sometimes a restraint on the wicked; therefore, whoever would laugh or argue it out of the world, without giving some equivalent for it, ought to be treated as a common enemy."
> —Lady Mary Wortley Montagu

How to Transcend the Loneliness of Mourning
Express your pain to others and allow tears to lessen your anguish.

If you're experiencing intense grief because of the death of a loved one, or are heartbroken over a cruel divorce, breakup, or abandonment, the healing process begins by communicating your sorrow openly. Weeping also can be a crucial and healthy part of the mourning process that will allow you to express the impact of your loss. Talking about your sorrow to others is important, too. Speaking of your emotional pain to trusted listeners will help reduce some of the profound numbness and aloneness that you shouldn't keep bottled up inside.

If you avoid the weeping and expressive stages of your mourning and refuse to accept the reality of your loss, internalizing and smothering your real feelings, you will prolong your grief. That may result in long-term loneliness, alienation, and depression. The denial of grief will also distort your sense of reality, keep you locked in the remorseful past, and poison most of your chances for future happiness because of the fragmented thinking it will produce.

Grief does have its beneficial aspects. By working through its major emotional components—shock, denial, anger, guilt, realization of permanent loss, and eventual acceptance—you will be ready to advance to another, more hopeful stage of life. As painful as grief may be at first, recognize that it will not last forever, and that when you complete your grieving process, you will emerge stronger and more self-reliant because you triumphed over an extremely difficult setback. If you're currently immobilized by your grief, and don't believe that you'll be able to withstand one additional moment of sorrow, loss, and emotional suffering, reach into your past. Try to recall another painful experience that left you numb, wounded, and depressed. Remember how you found the inner strength and the courage to go on with your life. Time did heal your wound.

The best way to overcome the loneliness of mourning is to take the focus off yourself by concentrating your energies on new endeavors. Make a positive effort to reach out and connect with other people. You'll suddenly discover that your old identity, the one that was attached to your loss and suffering, has been replaced by a new and stronger identity, confirming that life is meaningful again.

In this section, determine what steps you can undertake to release the loneliness of your heartache and grief.

(Example: "Everyone I see reminds me of Kim. I get crazy when I picture Kim being with someone else. My obsessive thoughts are driving me crazy and making me so very lonely. I've got to accept the reality of this breakup, and realize that this broken relationship will be replaced by a better one. I'll have one more good cry to complete my mourning process and then try to start dating again.")

_____

_____

_____

_____

_____

_____

"Oh, then indulge thy grief, nor fear to tell
 the gentle source from whence thy sorrows flow!
Nor think it weakness when we love to feel,
Nor think it weakness what we feel to show."
—William Cowper

How to Overcome the Loneliness of the Workplace
Find employment that builds social connections and promotes teamwork.

The modern work environment—the place where you'll probably spend a third of your life producing goods or services to earn a living—can be made an important Loneliness Remover tool. That's because some innovative companies have evolved into surrogate families to help offset the social instability caused by urban alienation, fragmented families, and the depersonalization of contemporary living. These companies reinforce the feeling of family in the workplace through picnics, intramural sports events, employee choirs, camera and hiking clubs, and other shared endeavors.

A caring workplace is the best defense against worker alienation in a changing world and can even form the basis of a substitute family structure when traditional links no longer exist.

A good work environment, where team spirit is emphasized, will produce new friendships that extend after working hours as well. If you are happy on your job—and feel recognized by management—you will not leave that job easily, especially if your coworkers have also become your friends.

In a noncaring work environment, your on-the-job loneliness will be heightened because you won't feel a sense of belonging, and you may be prohibited from speaking honestly to your boss. And even though you're within arm's reach of fellow employees, you'll always feel like an insignificant cog lost inside a large organization because you lack purpose, prestige, and social involvement. You're lonely because you don't enjoy your work.

You may also be lonely if you have mismatched work skills. If you're a sensitive person who likes working with people, but are employed in a subdued technical environment, you may want to reevaluate your work choice.

In this section, determine whether your job is a source of loneliness, and list steps you can take to end alienation in your workplace.

(Example: "My home life is lonely and this job makes me even lonelier because no one knows I exist. I need a people-oriented job where I can also make new friends. Let me try either waitressing or car-rental sales.")

_____
_____
_____
_____
_____
_____

"In order that people may be happy in their work, three things are needed: They must be fit for it. They must not do too much of it. And they must have a sense of success in it."
—John Ruskin

Why Excessive TV Viewing Will Prolong Your Loneliness
It is an isolating buffer that discourages social interaction.

Excessive TV viewing will increase alienation, fuel low self-worth, and prevent the buildup of personal and social skills needed to combat loneliness. Deepening isolation will occur because heavy TV watching is a hollow, detached, and passive one-way experience that will not provide you with live connections to other people.

For the unattached who need to link up with others, habitual TV watching is an electronic anti-intimacy buffer that will eventually transform you into a lonely voyeur. You'll spend your nightlife viewing the make-believe exploits of TV characters instead of reaching out to real people to maximize your own potential.

Moderate TV watching has its redeeming and informational value. It can help you become a more knowledgeable conversationalist and current-affairs expert, which will assist you in socializing on dates or at parties.

Not only will too much TV viewing tune you out of the real world, but it will also leave you with an unreal and distorted view of life that will further weaken your self-esteem. You will be comparing yourself to the fantasy-world characters who appear on your home screen—the Super-Rich, the Super-Greedy, the Super-Attractive, the Super-Strong, and the Super-Achievers—and you'll suffer from additional ego deflation after turning off your television set to face your own humble and lonely reality.

Breaking free of your isolating addiction to TV watching will reward you with an enlarged social arena that will allow new people-connection possibilities to enter your life. It will also sharpen your social skills and provide you with the results-oriented momentum to triumph over boredom, shyness, and rejection.

In this section, list three people-connection alternatives to replace your weeknight TV-viewing habits, and one community-service endeavor that will reduce your weekend addiction to TV watching.

(Example: "I'm giving up The Cosby Show *for a night out with Weight Watchers,* Monday Night at the Movies *for an adult education course, and* Miami Vice *for a church study group. I'll spend Saturdays as an American Red Cross volunteer helping the local blood drive."*)

(1) _____

(2) _____

(3) _____

"The value of life lies not in the length of days; but in the use we make of them: a man may live long, yet get little from life. Whether you find satisfaction in life depends not on your tale of years, but on your will."
—Michel de Montaigne

How to Meet Friends You Still Haven't Met
Friendships grow easily with people who share your common interests.

The world is full of friends you still haven't met, but it's up to you to make the move to meet them, because they're out there trying to meet you. It doesn't matter how young or old you are to begin building new friendships. Your soon-to-be friends are waiting for you to show up in night classes, support groups, antique and hobby shows, volunteer organizations, athletic events, cooking workshops, church-sponsored activities, and whatever other pursuits interest you. Friendships will form more easily with those people who share your common interests and similar life-style.

Those friends you still haven't met may be a little lonely, too, because some of their friends may have moved away, or they might have outgrown previous relationships.

You know how to push through the shyness hurdles to begin a conversation (page 19), but it's equally important that you not let your potential friends slip out of your life because you forgot about some of the basics of building a friendship. Here's what you should always remember in starting a brand-new friendship:

- Don't inject any negativity or pessimism into your beginning conversations, and for heaven's sake, let your newfound friends do most of the talking. Become a nurturing and caring listener, and people will want to spend more time with you; the attention you provide makes them feel good about themselves.
- Don't be boastful, prying, or self-involved when new friends ask you about your life and interests—and be open to making friends with someone of the opposite sex.
- Be willing to make friends with people of different cultural and social backgrounds. They'll broaden your friendship possibilities and strengthen your emotional outlook.

Step by step, your fledgling relationships will continue to grow. Perhaps you'll meet for lunch or supper and even attend a party or lecture together. You'll also use the telephone to help cement the friendship when you don't have the chance to meet in person.

There may come a time when your relationship with others develops strains—if you and your friends express dissimilar views on a touchy topic, for instance. If that's the case, make sure that all concerned agree to disagree over that issue and that your disagreements are healthy differences that will not harm your friendship.

In this section, propose three results-oriented actions you can initiate to help bring you closer to the new friends you still haven't met.

(Example: "I pledge to take the focus off myself the next time I get an opportunity to begin a conversation with a possible new friend, and I won't complain about my personal problems. The best place to begin meeting my kind of friends will probably be the Meadowbrook Horse Show. I'm at my best around horses—and I'd like to meet other horse lovers.")

(1) _____

(2) _____

(3) _____

"I find friendship to be like wine, raw when new, ripened with age, the true old man's milk and restorative cordial."

—Thomas Jefferson

Why the Search for Perfection Can Increase Loneliness
Unless you balance your expectations, you may never get close to someone.

Searching for the absolutely perfect partner—the one with the right height, weight, appearance, earnings, education, age, and cultural background—is a self-destructive pursuit that may impede your happiness. Perfectionism will actually prolong your loneliness because the quest for your idealized partner will make every other available person in the world seem unacceptable or inappropriate. And if you insist on maintaining your inflexible standards, it may indicate that you're somehow afraid of intimacy and are using your perfectionist needs either to hide or to remain unloved and unattached.

A word to the wise: Unless you modify your rigid expectations of a future partner, you may be sentencing yourself to a lifetime of social and emotional loneliness.

To push through your perfectionist barrier and open yourself to new possibilities of inner comfort through a fulfilling relationship, you could modify your requirements for a partner. That smart decision would allow more people to enter your life. It would also demonstrate that your self-worth and happiness are not dependent on another person's attainments.

In this section, list the essential physical, social, and emotional traits your ideal partner should possess. Then ask yourself whether you are setting your expectations unrealistically high, and where and how you could modify your expectations to find happiness with another person.

(Example: "I've spent the last nine years looking for a red-haired, sensitive lawyer—who is rich, athletic, handsome, unmarried, a hunk, a poet, a vegetarian skydiver, and ten years my senior. Guess what? A man like that doesn't exist in my community. If I let go of my unrealistic fantasy and date other men in my apartment complex, I'd probably have more luck meeting an available person. I don't have to marry rich to be happy!")

"The desire of perfection is the worst disease that ever afflicted the human mind."
—Louis, Marquis de Fontanes

How to Rekindle Old Friendships to Remove Loneliness
You'll never have to apologize to an old friend for not keeping in touch.

You may have an untapped reservoir of old friendships formed during your childhood and high school years that are special enough to stand the test of time. These friends represent a powerful source of spiritual and emotional strength to help you defeat loneliness. And even though time, distance, and personal priorities may have separated you from these special people, some things will never change about your old friends. They will always be there to provide you with compassion, support, and intimacy as they did during an earlier and different time in your life. And regardless of your current status, disappointments, or achievements, old friends will never be judgmental.

Old friends understand the difficulty of keeping in touch, and it's relatively easy to revitalize an old relationship. Just reach out and dial that old friend's number, reintroduce yourself, and then tap into some past mutual memories that should bring a smile to both of you. Your friendship will rekindle itself from that point. Remember that old friends need to hear from you as much as you need to hear from them. That's why your friendships originally took hold and blossomed.

Rekindling an old friendship is comparable to going on a fun-filled treasure hunt. If you're still living in your hometown, take out your old high school or college yearbook and make a list of all those special people you'd like to welcome back into your life. Use the telephone as your direct lifeline to track down those old friends. If you're living in a different part of the country, removed from these friends, have a telephone operator help track down those significant other people. Attend your next class reunion to find them. If you initially experience difficulty locating your old friends, contact their relatives. They might enjoy hearing from you. If you live out of your hometown, send away for the telephone directory. It should provide you with an abundance of information about old friends. Another good method for tracing people is to write a letter to the editor of the community newspaper where you're concentrating your efforts. Most newspapers will publish your request in their Letters to the Editor section as a personal favor.

In this section, list the names of three old friends you'd like to have back again in your life and record the steps you'll take to get in touch with them.

(Example: "I'm going to call the parents of my former high school cheerleader friend to help me find out where she's living these days. She was a really special person in my life. I'll try her hometown telephone operator for a start. We always had such great laughs together. I could use some now.")

(1) _____

_____

(2) _____

_____

(3) _____

_____

"In the life of a young man the most essential thing of happiness is the gift of friendship."
—Sir William Osler

Why Sharing Your Home Removes Loneliness
You'll have instant companionship and an extended network of friends.

Sharing your house or apartment with an appropriate other person—someone who is comfortable with your values, life-style, age range, and personal chemistry—is a fast and practical way to end your loneliness.

The appropriate home-sharer can provide you with built-in companionship, the beginnings of a new friendship, and the possibility of an extended network of other friends. In addition, you'll have monthly rental income to reduce your mortgage or rental payments—and you may find someone to share the chores.

Home-sharing does have some drawbacks that must be considered carefully, including the loss of privacy and perhaps reduced access to your telephone, kitchen, bathroom, or television in smaller homes. You may also have to shop and clean for two unless you draw up a contract in advance that defines the exact home-sharer responsibilities in your household.

And whether you choose a home-sharer of the same or the opposite sex, you should create your own checklist of personal preferences that you require of a home-sharer, such as the following: Would you want a roommate who smokes? Do you want to share your home with someone who runs a small business under your roof? Will you be comfortable with a home-sharer who is an artist or a musician? Could you live with an alcoholic or drug user?

If you believe your household has room for an appropriate home-sharer—and you're willing to give up some loss of control and privacy in your home in exchange for companionship with the right person—you're ready to reduce your loneliness.

In this section, prepare a classified advertisement listing your precise needs in a home-sharer. Describe who you are and what you're looking for. Don't include your home address, but provide a telephone number to help you screen out inappropriate candidates.

Also, before making a final commitment, establish your own provisions for immediate eviction should incompatibilities surface, and create your own rules for security deposit and reimbursement for any damages.

   (Example: "FEMALE HOME-SHARER NEEDED—*Professional woman with 2-bedroom apartment seeks same over 30. No smokers, overnight guests or parties, night-shift workers, or pets. Should like books and Japanese food. Near Fort Riley, Kansas. $350 rent includes utilities and indoor swimming pool. Call 000-0000."*

"Two may talk and one may hear, but three cannot take part in a conversation of the most sincere and searching sort."

—Ralph Waldo Emerson

Why Casual Sex Can Prolong Your Loneliness
It may leave you feeling deprived of love and lower your self-esteem.

If you're serious about bringing your loneliness to a happy ending, consider avoiding casual sexual encounters. These activities seldom provide real emotional involvement and are rarely accompanied by lasting love, caring, or intimacy. Sometimes casual sex can be tempting to the lonely because it seems to promise immediate involvement, but it may actually lower your sense of self-worth and leave you feeling emptier because someone wanted only a passing physical experience at your emotional expense. Exposure to casual sex, void of commitment and any long-term emotional sharing, may continue to produce shattered dreams and more loneliness because those experiences can prevent you from meeting an appropriate partner to begin a lasting romantic involvement.

There is an alternative to the hasty cycle of casual sex. It means taking the time to build a genuine emotional attachment, complete with trust and mutual respect, before moving into a full-fledged physical relationship. This will actually heighten your enjoyment of lovemaking and produce a stable foundation on which to continue building a permanent attachment.

In this section, decide for yourself whether sex without intimacy will provide you momentum to create a long-term nurturing emotional involvement, or if the rewards are greater when you develop intimacy before sex.

(Example: "I think I'm really falling for David, but we've only had a few dates since we met last month. Maybe if we go on that hiking trip next weekend with the gang it would be a good way to spend more time together just being friends. I don't want to get carried away like I did with Frank, then wake up to discover we only have a physical relationship and nothing else in common.")

"Whoever lives true life, will love true love."
—Elizabeth Barrett Browning

Why You Should Detach from a Lonely Friendship
It may be a liability that is no longer close or fulfilling.

Unfortunately, not all friendships stay the same. Some friendships may actually increase your loneliness—and turn into bona fide liabilities—if they fail to provide you with the mutual exchange of comfort, respect, companionship, and good feeling.

Detaching from a friendship that has become stale or one-sided and unfulfilling can be a sad and remorseful experience because of the shared memories of other, happier times. However, by choosing to remain in a relationship that you've probably outgrown and that is no longer mutually rewarding, you run the risk of further emotional loss and depression.

Sometimes a stagnant friendship can be revitalized if the other party is made to realize that his or her behavior has seriously weakened the relationship. However, human nature being what it is, most people will not admit that they skimp on emotional support or the sharing aspect of friendship, and so they may also be ready to move away from you.

Asking yourself the following questions may help you determine if your friendship is contributing to your loneliness.

• Are you on the receiving end of a negative and critical attitude because someone is uncomfortable with your new growth, aspirations, or achievements?

• Are you lonely in a friendship because you feel the other person has undergone a personality change?

• Are you lonely in a friendship because the support and nurturing you once received have turned into an empty obligation?

• Are you lonely in a friendship because the relationship was unable to stand the test of time but you're afraid to let it go?

• Are you lonely in a friendship because you've postponed taking steps to meet new people who share common interests and who may provide you with the nurturing companionship that you've always provided for others?

Perhaps it's time to begin breaking away from this

friendship and find new people who will accept you for who you are. In this section, describe a friendship that may be making you lonely and explain how you plan to resolve that relationship.

(Example: "Vanna used to be my best friend in high school and college, and during the last five years in business. We were the liveliest team that Kansas City ever saw. All she does now is stay home on weekends and watch TV, and chain-smoke between drinks. She always criticizes the men I date. Our friendship isn't fun anymore. I'm lucky that I've made some new friends at the camera class to connect with.")

_____

_____

_____

_____

_____

"Today is not yesterday: we ourselves change; how can our Works and Thoughts, if they are always to be the fittest, continue always the same? Change, indeed, is painful; yet ever needful; and if Memory have its force and worth, so also has Hope."

—Thomas Carlyle

How to Avoid Loneliness in Retirement
Find new interests, new paths to friendship, and new sources of self-fulfillment.

New retirees may be responsible for creating their own loneliness—and subsequent post-retirement blues—if they fail to replace the continuity of social contacts and sense of achievement their jobs formerly provided. Retirement can be extremely lonely and disappointing for men and women who formed strong personal identities through their work. Retirement can strip them of their purpose, their identity, and the motivation to go on with their lives. Other factors that produce loneliness in retirement are the realities of less money, reduced aspirations, and the feelings of being isolated from younger generations.

Retirement doesn't have to end in loneliness. The secret for an abundant social and emotional life in retirement is to transfer the best of your pre-retirement skills and abilities into your new leisure pursuits. That switch-over will ensure the same feelings of pride, accomplishment, and belonging you formerly received from your workplace experiences—even if you perform those same activities on a volunteer or part-time basis.

The rest of your new time in retirement will be allocated to cultivating new relationships, pursuing hobbies and athletic activities, and perhaps even signing up for adult education courses, where you'll meet more new people. Retirement can be a period of rebirth if you create an action blueprint that includes the new goals and personal priorities you think will bring self-sufficiency and fulfillment to your life as a retiree.

In this section, draw up that special blueprint for your post-retirement happiness. Include a plan for making new friendships and continuing a connection to your former line of work if that strengthens your self-esteem and sense of belonging, and consider whether you would enjoy contributing your services to help others.

(*Example:* "When I leave Waterloo to begin my retirement in Sarasota, I'm going to hold on to my sense of identity by doing part-time nursing. I'm going to stay involved with the church, and take college courses to meet new people. I'm just too good to remain holed up in a retirement village without having a say about managing my own life.")

_____
_____
_____
_____
_____

"True happiness is of a retired nature, and an enemy to pomp and noise; it arises, in the first place, from the enjoyment of one's self; and, in the next, from the friendship and conversation of a few select companions."
—Joseph Addison

How Temporary Work Can Help You Find New Friends
It will end your social isolation and boost your self-esteem.

Signing up for temporary employment is another smart anti-loneliness action that can provide you with many new people-connection opportunities. Here's why: If you're new to the job marketplace, or are about to re-enter it after completing other responsibilities, temporary employment may be your shortcut to either career or emotional rewards.

Not only can temporary work assignments increase your visibility in many different companies, on a daily, weekly, or monthly work schedule, but you'll also be able to determine almost immediately whether you have found a nurturing job or have landed in a very lonely workplace. At the same time, you should also be able to determine within a very short period whether the chances of meeting interesting new people are in your favor.

If you find the working conditions unfavorable to your long-term objectives, by changing your temporary work assignment you can create another brand-new opportunity for a better working and social environment.

Regardless of the type of work you do, temporary employment agencies can easily match your work skills with an appropriate employer. Temporary work will also boost your self-esteem—especially if you've been out of the job market for a while. It will sharpen your job-searching skills and strengthen your sense of self-worth and independence. Should you find that perfect job—a warm company complete with plenty of friendly co-workers—you might obtain a permanent position with that employer if you strive to make a good impression. In fact, your temporary employment agency might even earn an extra commission fee, paid by your new employer, if you decide to secure that permanent position.

In this section, examine whether the possibility of temporary work—which involves contact with many people in many different companies—is a practical way for you to get to know new people. Listings for most temporary employment agencies can be found in your local or regional telephone directories.

(Example: "It's really time to leave this dull secretarial typing pool and move to an exciting workplace where I can meet lots of available men. I'm signing up for temporary work. If I ask for specific assignments at military bases, police stations, medical schools, and construction companies, the odds of meeting available men will really jump in my favor.")

_____
_____
_____
_____
_____
_____
_____

"Work is a cure for all the maladies and miseries that ever beset mankind—honest work, which you intend getting done."

—Thomas Carlyle

How to Use Personal Ads to Remove Your Loneliness
They provide a direct link to intimacy with the appropriate partner.

Using the classified sections of newspapers and magazines is a highly effective method to meet new friends and romantic partners. Personal ads are efficient because they reach broad audiences, bypass the uncertainties of singles bars, and let you avoid the high start-up costs for membership in health clubs, video dating groups, and other endeavors that charge fees to bring the unattached together.

Properly written and placed personal ads have considerable Loneliness Remover clout because they put you in the catbird seat to receive mail from people who want specifically to meet you. You're in complete control because you decide whom to meet by sorting through the responses. Your advertisement will also guide you through shyness, rejection, and isolation hurdles by delivering your message directly to the pool of potential mates you're seeking to meet.

Writing a personal ad is relatively simple and requires complete self-honesty to produce the results you want.

The correct ad will also serve to fend off any inappropriate responses. The process begins with a brief self-assessment that will serve as your calling card: Who are you—sex, age, race, marital status—and what are your specific needs in a potential romantic partner?

Are you looking for a marriage partner or a casual companion, an intellectual, butcher, outdoors person, gourmet devotee, or financially secure business executive? Include this information in your advertisement. If you need to fine-hone your personal attributes to describe yourself in the ad, refer to the completed sections on self-image, self-confidence, and being your own best friend.

The more publications you advertise in, the more responses you'll attract. And if you place your personal ad in special-interest publications—physicians' magazines, nursing publications, legal journals, computer newspapers, hot-rod and racing magazines—your advertisement will reach the exact type of audience and person you want to connect with. Never publish your home address or telephone number in a classified advertisement. Use commonsense discretion also in selecting a safe public place to meet with the respondents to your ad. Weed out machine-copied responses to your advertisements and watch out for computer-generated letters. Multiple-submission letters may indicate a lack of serious intent or, conversely, extreme desperation.

In this section, prepare a twenty-five- to forty-word personal ad that specifies your goals, needs, and interests, and select one local and one special-interest publication that will carry your message to your intended target audience.

(*Example:* "FUN-LOVING NURSE, *31, and single mother—who loves camping, cooking, and commitment—seeks employed outgoing man who enjoys life, sharing, Elvis Presley movies, and church attendance. Seeking good-humored man between 30 and 40." This advertisement will run in the* Houston Chronicle *and* The National Horseman.)

_____
_____
_____
_____
_____
_____

"The meeting of two personalities is like the contact of two chemical substances: if there is any reaction, both are transformed."

—Carl Gustav Jung

How to Avoid Being Lonely in a Relationship
Express your true feelings as the first step toward more intimacy.

If you're lonely in a relationship because you're being deprived of intimacy, nurturing, and communication, an open expression of your true feelings will either help rekindle that passionless romance or help prepare you to leave it. Opening up to your partner with the important message that you're lonely in the relationship is the key step to restore the wonderful physical and emotional feelings that you once had.

An open and obliging partner—someone who cares about your love, welfare, and happiness—will welcome your honesty and will work together with you to recapture the intimacy missing from your relationship.

A closed and unobliging partner—someone who is selfish, withholding, unappreciative, and perhaps inappropriate for you—will view your need for intimacy and communication as a burden and personal imposition, thus denying your emotional needs.

Asking yourself the following questions may help you determine some of the reasons you may be experiencing loneliness in your relationship.

- Are you lonely in a relationship because you suffer from low self-esteem and fear even greater loneliness if you disengage from an unsatisfactory relationship?

- Are you lonely in a relationship because you don't have any outside interests—or friends outside of your relationship—to reinforce your identity and self-worth as a multifaceted person? Are you too dependent on your mate to fulfill all of your social and emotional needs?

- Are you lonely because you have outgrown your relationship but continue to remain in it because you're afraid to strike out on your own—and because you don't have the assurance of finding a replacement?

- Are you lonely in a relationship because the burdens of your work—and perhaps your mate's job-related stresses—have sapped the vibrancy of your once strong romance?

- Are you lonely in a relationship because your partner is fearful of intimacy and attachment—and refuses to fulfill any of your long-term emotional needs?

Other loneliness-producing factors can easily be added to this list, but it's important to remember that if you and your partner communicate your loneliness to each other and schedule time together to resolve the problem of lack of intimacy, you can rekindle that relationship. Then strengthen your bond by doing interesting things together.

In this section, determine some of the reasons you may be lonely in a relationship, and list some of the actions you can take to correct the situation.

(Example: "Jonas never talks to me when he comes home after work, and I never see him on weekends because he spends all of his time rebuilding old cars. I'm going to tell him to make room for me in his life—otherwise this relationship is over. I don't deserve to give all of my love and attention and receive nothing in return!")

_____

_____

_____

_____

_____

_____

"Everything begins from loneliness."
—John Erskine

How to Avoid the Holiday Cycle of Loneliness and Depression
Plan activities that will bring you in contact with other people.

The major holidays—and their mandatory emphasis on group merriment and collective rejoicing—impose emotional hardships on men and women who are unloved, unattached, or not looped into the mainstream of family, friendship, or support group networks. Suicide statistics mount dramatically among the unattached, who may view their unfilled lives as an overwhelming disappointment during holiday festivities.

The following strategies are recommended to help the unattached defeat the emotional sabotage of feeling unloved during peak holiday times. If the suggestions are not applicable in your particular situation, you can share them with someone who may need them.

If any are relevant to your needs, attend open-to-the-public meetings of Alcoholics Anonymous, Overeaters Anonymous, Gamblers Anonymous, Debtors Anonymous, Emotions Anonymous (P.O. Box 4245, St. Paul, MN 55104), or Al-Anon, all of which are listed in your telephone directory. These extraordinary self-help organizations sometimes hold round-the-clock meetings during holiday periods—and you'll always feel part of a very special and extended loving family.

Revitalize an old friendship that you've neglected. Remember that everyone experiences loneliness and needs to hear from good friends like you.

Plan activities that will help other people—and that will also bring you happiness. Visit a bedridden person who will be elated by your presence. Donate food and clothing to someone less fortunate than you. Or adopt a new friend and loyal companion at your nearby animal shelter during the Christmas holidays.

Create a holiday support group to help the unattached get through that emotionally difficult period. State right up front that you're lonely and don't want to remain that way. Discuss real problems. Your candor will serve as an inspiration to others. Plan this support group in advance, and use the personals section in the newspapers to reach others. Ask a church, synagogue, or public service agency to provide you with free or low-cost meeting rooms.

Reach out to a priest, minister, rabbi, social worker, or concerned classmate or teacher and tell that person you're going to be pretty isolated and vulnerable during the holiday period. Perhaps you can be matched up with someone else who will be coping with the same set of circumstances—and you may end up with a newfound friend.

Be good to yourself and avoid the downbeat effects of alcohol and other chemical depressants taken during the holiday period.

In this section, plan three people-oriented actions to help you defeat the menacing holiday loneliness syndrome—especially if you are down and unattached and may be feeling particularly vulnerable.

(Example: "I know a few other people who don't have anyone to connect with around the holiday period. I'm going to invite them to my house for an evening of fellowship and support. Then I'm going to a free open meeting of Overeaters Anonymous to find out why I eat so much food whenever I feel lonely.")

(1) _____

(2) _____

(3) _____

"Not one can harm the man who does himself no wrong."

—St. John Chrysostom

How to Stop the Loneliness of Overdrinking or Overeating
Meet fellowships that will love you as you learn to love yourself.

Chronic loneliness can be either the cause or the effect of destructive overdrinking and excessive overeating, as you hide from your feelings of low self-worth and alienation. Two extraordinary self-help groups will show you how to make your life joyful and enthusiastic again.

The two nurturing fellowships—Alcoholics Anonymous (AA) and Overeaters Anonymous (OA)—have no dues, fees, or compulsory attendance requirements. In return for collective companionship, guidance, and emotional bonding, both AA and OA will provide you with the life-rebuilding tools to show you how to stop drinking or end compulsive overeating, and defeat loneliness. Both organizations share a common healing tradition consisting of a no-nonsense philosophy of twelve humanistic healing guidelines—including a belief in God—that reshape and rebuild lives through spiritual and emotional growth.

The fellowships are made up of mainstream people from all walks of life who attend daily or weekly meetings and openly share their uphill experiences of triumphing over their food or drinking disorders—and beating loneliness.

Before you make a decision about AA or OA, attend at least three open meetings to see how the loneliness recovery process produces results. Also, go to meetings in different sites until you find the right group for you. AA and OA meetings are held in the USA and Canada, and elsewhere throughout the world. Meetings are either "open" or "closed" to the general public, and the principle of complete anonymity ensures widespread trust and sharing among the members.

Both organizations endorse daily contact with an AA or OA sponsor—someone who was successful in arresting his or her drinking or eating problem. That daily contact reduces alienation, builds self-esteem, and strengthens the personal commitment to lead a nondestructive life. Being a member of either fellowship means you will always have the love of a caring and extended support network. You'll never be alone—unless you choose to be. In fact, both fellowships are so strong that if you can't get to a meeting on your own, a volunteer might drive you back and forth from your home if you reach out and ask for that help.

You can find out about AA meeting places and times by calling the local AA chapter listed in your telephone directory or by writing to: AA General Services, P.O. Box 459, Grand Central Station, New York, NY 10163.

Likewise, OA meeting places and schedules can be found by calling the local chapter or by writing to: Overeaters Anonymous, World Service Organization, 4025 Spencer Street, Suite 203, Torrance, CA 90504.

In this section, determine whether an exploratory visit to an AA or OA meeting would improve your emotional performance by reducing your loneliness-generating addictions.

(Example: "The only time I'm not lonely is when I'm drunk in a bar making a fool out of myself. I've lost my self-respect. I think I'll go to an AA meeting and learn how others got over their drinking and loneliness problems.")

"The spirit of self-help is the root of all genuine growth in the individual."

—Samuel Smiles

Why Adult Education Courses Yield New Friends
They promote a bonding forum similar to high school or college experiences.

Signing up for an adult education course is a fun, practical, nonthreatening way to meet new friends—and it's fairly inexpensive. It will provide people-connection advantages which, though not usually discussed in school catalogs, are very important for those wanting to expand their friendships. The possibilities offered by adult education courses are many. You don't have to feel self-conscious about your age, because most adult education courses are comprised of mainstream people representing all age categories. You can avoid having to stake out singles lectures, singles bars, health clubs, food market aisles, screaming primal-therapy encounter sessions, athletic or cultural events you don't enjoy, and dating-agency recommendations in endless forays to meet new friends or romantic partners.

There's also something very special about meeting others in an adult education course: You obviously have mutual interests. In many ways, it's similar to your friend-filled high school or college days, when it was so easy to meet others and form budding friendships between class breaks or in the cafeteria.

Here's how to ensure that you'll find the rewards, pleasures, and friendships you're seeking when you sign up for an adult education course:

1. Select courses that will promote the kind of lively classroom discussion that may carry over into a spontaneous coffee-shop group when class ends. Human behavior courses usually produce after-class discussions.

2. Don't sign up for any mass-lecture auditorium class. Such classes are uncomfortable, nonintimate, and noninteractive.

3. Select courses that maximize interaction between you and your classmates—and that offer stimulation, conversation, and the possibilities of spontaneous humor. Good choices include photography, acting, dancing, cooking, and foreign languages.

4. If possible, avoid those one-night "instant courses," because they'll reduce the chance for you to meet new

people. Weekly courses are your best bet to create new friendship opportunities.

In this section, obtain the name of your nearest adult education facility, and choose two courses that will give you pleasure and enjoyment, and connect you to other people.

(Example: "Dancing was always fun for me as a youngster, so I'm going to sign up for a contemporary dance workshop. And this course—'How to Talk to Your Plants'—sounds like a winner. I wonder what my plants and I will have to say to each other?")

_____

_____

_____

_____

_____

"That's what education means—to be able to do what you've never done before."
—George Herbert Palmer

Why Group Therapy Is a Powerful Remedy for Loneliness
The special-purpose family provides a base of encouragement and belonging.

Group therapy is a fast-working antidote to loneliness and is particularly effective for unattached persons—or those lonely in a relationship—who need the helping hand of a special-purpose or substitute-family group to reduce their loneliness. The group will provide its new member—who must be committed to learning and growing from the group process—with the companionship, interaction, and guidance to overcome the conditions that brought on the original loneliness.

In fact, the dynamics of group therapy interplay may also uncover some of the psychological reasons behind the long-term loneliness that conventional one-on-one counseling might have missed. That's because group members sometimes take on the role of brothers, sisters, and parents in a controlled healing environment, and members are able to transfer or elicit responses that might have remained buried in individual counseling discussions.

Group therapy is highly effective for the chronically shy and for those suffering from low self-esteem, because the substitute-family forum operates in a safe, nurturing environment. And in that process, all group members are encouraged to speak, contribute, and interact. Everyone receives group encouragement and acceptance—two important catalysts to emotional growth that build up the personal stamina needed to triumph over loneliness.

Group therapy also serves as a great equalizer in the loneliness healing process. New members learn that they are not really alone in their loneliness—and that their problems are really not unique.

To maintain its effectiveness, a group must be led and organized by a certified mental health facilitator. Information can be obtained by contacting your local mental health association. Avoid joining groups that specialize in screaming confrontation techniques. Always ask to become a member of a nurturing behavior-modification group. Special-purpose/substitute-family groups have a lifespan of about three months to two years, and will continue running indefinitely if the need exists. Group meetings are usually held weekly and cost about $25 for a two-hour session. Some medical plans cover costs for group therapy.

And although group therapy membership may not always bring an immediate end to your loneliness, it will provide you with newfound social and emotional coping skills, a community of your own—and many friendships formed within your group. You'll also develop a stronger outlook and the ultimate payoff of learning how to appreciate your own self-worth.

In this section, determine whether you need the emotional support of the group process to reduce your loneliness—and how you might pay for those services.

(Example: "I need to connect with others because I've been in total isolation since moving to Cedar Rapids. I've got no one here, and could use the support of a substitute family. I'll give up smoking to pay for group.")

_____
_____
_____
_____
_____

"Speech is civilization itself. The word, even the most contradictory word, preserves contact—it is silence which isolates."

—Thomas Mann

How Not to Suffer the Loneliness of an Alcoholic Relationship
Al-Anon will end your alienation and provide you with many new friends.

If you're one of the countless millions living in lonely suffering because you're involved with an active alcoholic—whether spouse, parent, relative, or friend—there is direct action you can take to remove your loneliness. Ask your local telephone operator to give you the nearest Al-Anon telephone number. This number will serve as your immediate link to a loving and nonjudgmental fellowship that will provide you with immediate hope, strength, and understanding to recover from your difficulties.

Al-Anon is not a flashy or high-visibility organization. It is a potent national and worldwide group that helps create countless modern-day emotional miracles for people who are lonely, abused, tormented, manipulated, or functionally immobilized because active alcoholics are a part of their lives. Al-Anon does not require any dues or membership fees, and there are no documents to sign. Expenses are met through small contributions taken at meetings.

Once you've made the call to your nearest Al-Anon center or attended your first meeting on your own, this healing fellowship will begin putting many new supportive friends into your life. These friends will show you how to cope with the loneliness and other adverse effects resulting from someone else's drinking problem. An amazing self-transformation will begin. The recovery and healing process will be shifted to you—and away from the alcoholic in your life. You'll be taught that your emotional survival is paramount and that you aren't responsible for another person's alcoholism. You'll also be taught by the loving Al-Anon fellowship that you didn't cause the other person's alcoholism, nor will *you* ever be able to cure it. Al-Anon rebuilds the human spirit and effectively strengthens self-esteem because it uses the successful twelve-step humanistic healing process developed by Alcoholics Anonymous (page 62), and because it is a wonderful catalyst for new emotional momentum.

At each Al-Anon meeting—filled with mainstream men and women and even teenagers from your community who are pledged to maintain an anonymous and confidential relationship at all times—members openly share their experience and their recovery. They talk about their problems—and what they're doing to detach themselves from someone else's destructive drinking caused by the disease of alcoholism. It's not easy to distance yourself from someone you love, but Al-Anon will provide you with the strength, courage, and companionship to do so. You'll never be alone in the Al-Anon fellowship: It was structured to form close bonds among members. Most of them will gladly exchange their telephone numbers with you if you need round-the-clock emotional support.

If an Al-Anon family group does not exist in your community, you can start your own if you can find one or more persons who want such a group because a problem drinker has affected their lives. Write to AFG Inc., P.O. Box 862, Midtown Station, New York, NY 10018, for free starter kits and other information.

If you're lonely and emotionally immobilized because of another person's destructive behavior not caused by alcoholism—whether physical abuse, mental cruelty, or nonstop addiction to other dangerous substances—quietly attend Al-Anon meetings on your own. Listen and learn at the meetings, and you, too, will find the courage and strength to pull away from a destructive relationship.

In this section, determine whether attending an Al-Anon meeting will help you overcome the loneliness and futility of being involved with a self-destructive addicted person.

(*Example:* "*History seems to be repeating itself. I was lonely as a child because both my parents were alcoholics, and the only attention I ever received was beatings. Now I'm involved with an alcoholic who is manipulating my life and is destroying whatever feeling of self-worth I have left. I must reach out to the Al-Anon friendship to strengthen my life!*")

"God, give us grace to accept with serenity the things that cannot be changed, the courage to change the things which should be changed, and the wisdom to distinguish the one from the other."
 —The Serenity Prayer, adapted from Reinhold Niebuhr

How to Defeat Teenage Loneliness
Take positive actions to connect with people who will respect you.

Every teenager's despair over personal isolation can be reversed for a happy ending—and the best way to achieve that goal is first to figure out why you're feeling lonely. Then you can take the appropriate actions to defeat your feelings of alienation and inadequacy. It is important to understand that those feelings are common among all teenagers. And most teenagers are pretty good at concealing it—even though their pain of loneliness may be similar to yours. Therefore, always remind yourself that your loneliness isn't really unique, and that it shouldn't make you feel different from others.

Following are some major reasons why you may be feeling lonely, as well as actions you can take to reduce those feelings.

If you're lonely because your school is too large, and your classes are too crowded and impersonal, pick out clubs and extracurricular activities that will allow you to develop better one-on-one relationships with both teachers and students. The choices are yours: It could be the school band, chorus, or student newspaper; a religious, hobby, or sports club; or a student organization that performs humanitarian services in your hometown. In no time at all, you'll see that you have created a very special place for yourself at school and that you now connect with others who share your similar interests. New friends will come more easily.

If you're lonely because other teenagers are not inviting you to their parties—or are refusing to let you become a member of their club or gang—one solution is to take a part-time job after school. You'll get a chance to meet some new people on the job who can develop into new friends. And the money you earn will provide you with a new feeling of self-reliance that will broaden your abilities to meet others. Turn to younger friends if you can't break into a clique or group of your peers. Younger friends will be admiring and pleased with your companionship because they're usually searching for older role models.

If you're lonely because your mother and father are divorced—and you're blaming yourself for that breakup or are feeling abandoned—talk to both parents about your feelings. Write them each a letter if the words are difficult to say, and then schedule a meeting with your guidance counselor for additional support. If you have difficulty relating to your guidance counselor, don't give up. Schedule an appointment with your local community mental health services facility. That's where you should find a trained counselor who may better understand your situation and provide you with the help you need. Those services are usually low-cost or free.

You're not to blame for your parents' divorce, and you might try to strengthen your relationship with other family members—aunts, uncles, grandparents—and sympathetic teachers.

If you're lonely and unhappy because you feel pressured to excel at school at all costs—and the burden is depriving you of time for companionship with your friends—tell your parents about the tensions and emotional pain they're inflicting on you. If they can't seem to understand, schedule a meeting with your guidance counselor. Outside intervention may be the only warning your family may heed.

If you're lonely because your parents or guardians are affected by alcoholism—and are hurting you or abusing your dignity—look for the Alateen telephone number in your local directory. You'll meet other teenagers facing similar problems, and together you'll find ways to protect yourself from your parents. You'll make new friends who will understand your special kind of loneliness. Alateen will show you how to develop a happier and fuller life.

And if you're lonely because you feel unattractive, abandoned, or betrayed by a close friend or a clique, don't keep those painful feelings locked up inside. You can work to overcome those difficult emotions, which sometimes are a normal part of growing up, by confiding in your parents, a clergyman, or anyone you feel close to, and by talking to sympathetic teachers and counselors. They'll understand your "cry for help" and will try to give you the emotional support and acceptance you need at this point in your life.

And no matter how bad you feel, don't even think about turning to drugs, alcohol, or sex to gain acceptance by others. That's really an action against yourself, which can destroy your self-esteem, damage your physical and emotional health, and set you up as a target of cruel gossip.

Your best defense against teenage loneliness is to take

positive actions that will put you in touch with others who will respect you and appreciate your personal dignity. In this section, complete your own list of actions you can take to reduce your teenage loneliness.

(Example: *"I'm suffering from two types of teenage loneliness. There's nobody special in my life and that group of kids never invites me to parties. I think I can make new friends if I join a few school clubs—and I might even meet my teenage dream. A part-time job might also be good for my ego!"*)

_____

_____

_____

_____

_____

"I confess to pride in this coming generation. You are working out your own salvation; you are more in love with life; you play with fire openly, where we did in secret, and few of you are burned!"

—Franklin D. Roosevelt

How to Avoid the Loneliness of Motherhood
Look for new kinds of connection strategies to end your isolation.

The loneliness of motherhood is a painful reality for many homebound women, isolated in either uncaring suburban communities or impersonal urban environments, who are dedicated to being with their young children full-time. A lonely mother's unhappiness may spill over into nonstop eating disorders or drinking problems, or perhaps even a "cry for help" sexual adventure that may bring further disenchantment to the marriage.

The loneliness may also become unmanageable—and may cripple a marriage—if a husband refuses to listen to a daily recounting of his wife's problems. His own negative feelings about the stress of his job may cause him to shut off sympathetic feelings for his lonely wife.

The loneliness of motherhood does not have to exist. The following are some immediate-action strategies that may help reduce maternal isolation and rebuild self-esteem.

1. Don't let your husband take your child-raising accomplishments for granted. Explain that your maternal life at home has become too lonely, monotonous, and stressful—and you both need to find common solutions to restore your happiness.

2. Schedule time away from your child or children by using a trusted baby-sitter or linking up with a baby-sitting cooperative. Use your new free time to do what you enjoy doing best.

3. Find someone to confide in about your feelings of isolation. And if you learn of other lonely mothers—or advertise to meet others—you'll have the resources to form your own support group.

4. If your presence at home is mandatory, consider starting a part-time home business that will bring you in daily contact with others and reinforce your self-worth. You may consider tutoring, word processing, light sewing, telephone answering, specialty cooking, or any other

home-based endeavor that provides you with dignity and self-acceptance.

5. Keep taking personal actions that will put you in contact with other people while also allowing you to continue your child-rearing. Enroll in part-time college study, become part-time cashier at a nearby business, or take up an exercise or dance class in the company of others.

6. If you've followed most of the recommendations listed above and still find yourself lonely in motherhood, contact a certified mental health practitioner who will work together with you to remedy your loneliness.

In this section, list several people-connection actions that will help you reduce the loneliness of motherhood in your present homebound environment.

(Example: "Staying at home with my young daughter does not satisfy all of my emotional needs. I'd feel less isolated if I could work out at my health club, have lunch with some of my single girlfriends, and sign up for a few fun college courses.")

___

"Life is mostly froth and bubble;
Two things stand like stone:
Kindness in another's trouble,
Courage in your own."
—Adam Lindsay Gordon

How Newspapers Can Help You Beat Loneliness
They are filled with information to help you connect with others.

Your hometown newspaper is one of the most effective and inexpensive ways to meet other people—and it doesn't matter whether you live in a small town or large city. If you read your local paper regularly—as well as any other periodical that covers your community—you'll be equipped with a near-limitless calendar of events that can be golden opportunities. Study the coverage of upcoming leisure, entertainment, and service events that are open to the public. Are they of interest to you? Would you enjoy a free lecture on local history, the debut of a regional artist, or a fund-raising auction to help homeless cats and dogs? Attend only the events that will provide you with a known comfort factor of predictability and familiarity; otherwise your decision to connect with others may be unrewarding and even counterproductive.

Next, examine the various notices of meeting schedules listed in your hometown paper to see which are open to the public. The organizations that are holding meetings want and need your participation—but you'll have to decide where your interests, talents, and needs fit best.

The movers and shakers in your community may be appealing for you to serve as a youth center volunteer, or to attend a church-sponsored homemaking class, or to join a local ecology group. There may be notices in your newspaper urging you to join the camera club, hiking club, or stamp club, and you may even be invited to a marriage-enrichment workshop or an Audubon Society slide presentation. And there are still more people-connection opportunities for you to consider: The local chess and bridge clubs are looking for new members; a drum and bugle marching band needs volunteers; support groups for adolescents, widows, single parents, or senior citizens are calling for new members. A hospice needs your support, and the local fire department and Red Cross chapter are looking for a few good men and women. An amateur theater group is putting on a free play, a new singles club is forming, and the Mayor's Office is holding a sensitivity workshop for divorced fathers.

The above are but a few samples of people-connection possibilities your hometown newspaper can provide. It's up to you to take the initiative, end your isolation, and decide where you can expect to receive a sense of belonging, recognition, and acceptance.

In this section, after looking at today's edition of your local newspaper, list three possible events that will help you connect with others. Then make a commitment to attend one of the three.

(Example: "The American Legion is hosting a local seminar on good citizenship, a senior citizens' group is staging a nutrition workshop, and a new singles club is holding its first mixer. I'll attend the seminar on good citizenship because that's a very special topic for me—and I'll be comfortable in that environment.")

(1) _____

(2) _____

(3) _____

"The joys of meeting pay the pangs of absence;
Else who could bear it?"
—Nicholas Rowe

How to Beat the Loneliness of Overspending
Turn to a fellowship that understands your problem.

If you're afflicted by the loneliness of overspending, you're probably buying expensive items you really don't want or need or can't afford. And even though you're short on funds, you may continue buying more expensive and unneeded items because those purchases may temporarily inflate your low self-worth—and provide you with a false emotional nourishment that denies your basic feelings of being unloved and alone.

The loneliness of overspending is a harmful compulsion that can even make your life lonelier, because as your shopping binges continue, your past-due bills become larger. You may even go deeper into debt—and begin borrowing from your friends, family, and coworkers—to buy more unneeded items as old creditors begin pursuing you. You'll eventually begin avoiding those who loaned you money, possibly those closest to you, and you might retreat further from the painful reality of your financial obligations, even becoming reclusive.

As time goes on, the loneliness of overspending may bring you shame, loss of friends, and an end to any respect you had from your family.

Don't despair. There's a powerful nurturing fellowship available to help you defeat the loneliness of overspending—and one that will bring many new friends into your life. It's called Debtors Anonymous, and it uses many of the results-oriented healing strategies developed by Alcoholics Anonymous (page 62) to help compulsive spenders and debtors win over their self-destructive spending.

Here's how that fellowship works: In meetings held at church halls or in other settings, men and women recount openly how their compulsive shopping or debts made their lives unmanageable. All sharing is confidential. The fellowship promotes an end to isolation, and recovery from the loneliness of compulsive spending and being in debt through the exchange of telephone numbers.

Debtors Anonymous also encourages members to keep budgets and daily records of expenses, to share their record-keeping activities with other fellowship members, and to become members of a Debtors Anonymous pressure group.

In a pressure group meeting, a newcomer is aided by two other fellowship members, one man and one woman, who will serve as confidants, peers, and understanding listeners to formulate living and financial strategies to help the newcomer repay all his or her debts.

The Debtors Anonymous fellowship does not believe in bankruptcy; it advocates repayment as the way to build self-esteem and to create a better and fuller life.

For more information on the nearest Debtors Anonymous meeting in your area, or on starting your own meetings, write to: Debtors Anonymous, General Service Board, P.O. Box 20322, New York, NY 10025.

In this section, determine whether a connection to the Debtors Anonymous fellowship will help you end the loneliness of overspending, or help you manage your growing debts.

(Example: "I can't handle my bills anymore, but I keep on buying jewelry and clothing I really can't afford and don't need, just so I can impress others. If I didn't feel so lonely, I might not shop compulsively. Perhaps a visit to the Debtors Anonymous fellowship will help overcome my feelings of loneliness and not being a whole person.")

_____

_____

_____

"He that gets out of debt grows rich."
—George Herbert

How to Beat the Loneliness of Machismo
Try taking the new masculine risks of self-improvement.

If you're like most men who have been taught since childhood to control your feelings—no matter how painful, punishing, or stressful they are—you may be suffering from the deep-rooted loneliness of machismo. No one ever bothered to tell you that your repressed anger—or suffocated feelings of pain upheld in the name of "tough guy" masculinity—may resurface elsewhere. Those misplaced feelings of frustration, loss, loneliness, and helplessness might reappear as misdirected rage that could trigger physical illness, nervous breakdowns, and unprovoked violence against others. But that destructive emotional cycle doesn't have to prevail any longer.

You can triumph over the loneliness of machismo—and being closed off to your feelings—by taking the following new masculine risks to improve your emotional performance and awareness:

The first new masculine risk requires letting go of your "no win" role of holding on to self-punishing emotional and physical standards—win-at-any-expense, suffer-for-any-cause priorities—that are defining your masculinity.

The second new risk is redefining your interpretation of masculinity and equating real manhood with the ability to express your emotional needs.

The third new risk means changing from being a solitary person and evolving into a sharing, nurturing, and compassionate friend and mate.

The fourth new risk is learning to tell others that you're lonely—and if you're rejected by your peers for expressing your needs, then it's time to begin making new friends (page 40).

The fifth new masculine risk involves deciding to join a behavior modification group, one that includes women members, and learning how to shake off the machismo emotional choke hold on your life. Your local mental health service, a social worker, or a clergyman can help you find an appropriate group therapy opportunity.

In this section, determine whether you're ready to leave the ranks of the loneliness of machismo, and suggest actions you can take to meet your real human needs.

(Example: "Why are men afraid to have honest conversation? All that sports talk in the office is leaving me dry. Why don't we talk about how distant our wives and our children feel to us? Why don't we talk about the burden of our high monthly mortgage payments—and why we ever agreed to them in the first place. I'm through with being out of touch and so repressed as a man; I'll join a co-ed therapy group to help me sort out my real feelings.")

_____

_____

_____

_____

_____

"Loneliness is never more cruel than when it is felt in close propinquity with someone who has ceased to communicate."

—Germaine Greer

Why It's Time to Throw Your Own Party
It's a celebration of your own self-acceptance and forges a link to others.

Now that you've completed most of the sections of the *Loneliness Remover* and have learned how to become your own best friend and a good friend to others, it's time to celebrate your achievements. You're going to throw a party that will serve as a confirmation of your personal growth, self-acceptance, and commitment to connect with others.

Throwing your own party shouldn't produce any anxiety because you will know most of the guests and will be doing the entertaining at home. Don't invite anyone you're not sure you like—and don't include any self-loathing critical types who could spoil your festive mood. Your decision to have a party will be a turning point in your social development: It will increase your self-esteem and heighten your popularity.

Your guest roster might include new friends you've made through adult education courses, interesting people who responded to your classified ad, someone you helped through difficult times, friendly coworkers, and rediscovered old friends from high school or college. You could also include a wonderful element of surprise for your party by asking all or some of your guests to invite one or more of their friends to your celebration. Don't become another victim of unrealistic expectations and projections by anticipating that your party will produce the long-awaited love of your life. That takes place only in fairy tales. Keep your objectives in perspective.

The rewards you'll receive from throwing your own party will be abundant. You'll create the opportunity to meet some interesting people you haven't met before. You may subsequently receive invitations to attend other parties, and you'll feel good because you produced a fun event that brought together some of your newest and oldest friends.

Plan your party at least four weeks in advance so that your intended guests have enough time to change their plans if your invitation conflicts with one of their previous commitments. And don't expect that everyone you invite will be able to attend your party. That's another unrealistic wish. All that matters is that you've taken the initiative to bring friends together for a party, and that you're no longer a bystander in planning your own entertainment.

In this section, determine whether you are ready to hold a party, and produce a tentative list of your guests. If your home is too small, or the party arrangements seem too complex, would it be easier for you to cohost the party with another friend and double your chances of meeting more new people?

(Example: "My living room can hold only fifteen people, but if I hold my party at Sophia's place, she can invite an equal number of her friends. Between the two of us, we could produce a really amazing guest list of interesting people, and that would probably result in invitations to lots of other parties.")

_____

_____

_____

_____

_____

"The friends of my friends are my friends."
—Unknown (French proverb)

To the Special People Who Read My Book
Promise me that you'll always try to connect with others.

I believe in your perseverance, your optimism, and your special goodness. I sincerely hope that your loneliness comes to an end after you have followed the guidelines of this book—and that you'll always reach out to other people who are lonely, and show them how to enrich their lives.

There are some personal insights about the Loneliness Remover process that I'd like to share with you. In the beginning, there will be times when you may experience self-doubt. Don't give in to it—and always remember how strong, special, and unique you are. Sometimes you may relive old feelings of abandonment and of not belonging. But remember that you're now equipped to find and create your own special place in the world, where you will be loved and accepted unconditionally. Take special actions to connect, join, and belong. No more feelings of nonacceptance for you.

There may come a moment in the people-connection process when you feel you want to just give up. That's natural. But you've come too far for that. Let's both work together to reduce your feelings of loneliness. All you have to do to succeed is keep a few promises made between the two of us.

- Promise me that you'll memorize and internalize all your self-esteem attributes completed in the beginning of *Loneliness Remover* until they become part of your consciousness.
- Promise me that you'll no longer give in to your self-condemning thoughts when you experience feelings of loneliness. You're too good and important for that.
- Promise me that you'll never surrender to shyness or rejection—and that you'll always make a special effort to keep a trusted listener in your life.
- And promise me that you'll always keep on keeping on. I promise you that the best is still to come.

—Michael Krawetz